The Four Seasons

Orlando Austin New York San Diego Toronto London

Visit *The Learning Site!*
www.harcourtschool.com

What Is a Season?

Is the weather the same all year long? In most places on Earth, the weather changes with the seasons. A **season** is a time of year.

There are four seasons. Which is your favorite?

One year has four seasons. The seasons are spring, summer, fall, and winter. The next year we have the same seasons. The order is the same. They form a pattern.

SEQUENCE What season comes after winter?

Spring

Spring is the season after winter. In spring, the weather is warm. It may rain a lot. There are more hours of daylight in spring than in winter.

Plants get more warmth, light, and rain in spring. They may grow new leaves. They may grow flowers, too.

Many plants begin to grow in spring.

In spring, deer feed on new plants.

New plants are food for many animals. It is easy to find many kinds of food in spring. It is a good time for animals to have their young.

Focus Skill **MAIN IDEA AND DETAILS** **What is the weather like in spring?**

Summer

Summer is the season after spring. It is warmer in summer than in spring. Summer has many hours of daylight.

The heat in summer helps plants grow. Many plants grow fruits.

In summer, young animals can find lots of food. They grow bigger.

It is summer and the berries are ready to eat!

In summer, animals find ways to stay cool.

It may be very hot in summer. Animals find ways to stay cool. Some cool off in water.

Fast Fact

Elephants flap their ears to stay cool in hot weather.

Some animals lose fur so their coats are lighter! People wear lighter clothes to stay cool.

MAIN IDEA AND DETAILS **Name ways summer is different from spring.**

Fall

The season after summer is **fall**. There are less hours of daylight in fall than in summer. Fall is cooler than summer. People wear heavier clothes in fall to keep warm.

In some places, leaves on plants change color and fall to the ground. Fruits get ripe. People pick the fruits and eat them. Animals eat the fruits, too.

Leaves on some trees change color in fall.

Squirrels stay busy in the fall, storing food for winter.

In fall, some animals store food to eat in winter. Other animals migrate. Animals that **migrate** move to new places to find food.

Fast Fact

Sometimes squirrels forget where they stored their food. When they can not find the seeds they stored, those seeds grow into new plants.

CAUSE AND EFFECT **Why do some animals migrate?**

Winter

Winter is the season after fall. Of the four seasons, winter has the fewest hours of daylight. Some places are very cold in winter. Snow may fall. People in cold places wear heavy clothes.

Many plants have no leaves in winter. Some plants stay green. Many plants die. Some plants stay alive but do not grow until it is warm again.

When it is cold, food can be hard to find. Some animals eat food that they stored in fall. Some go to sleep until spring!

MAIN IDEA AND DETAILS What happens to plants in winter?

Pine trees stay green even in winter.

Summary

A year has four seasons. The seasons are spring, summer, fall, and winter. Weather changes over the seasons.

Glossary

fall The season after summer where the air begins to get cooler (3, 8, 9, 10, 11)

migrate To move to a new place to find food (9)

season A time of year. A year has four seasons. (2, 3, 4, 6, 8, 10, 11)

spring The season after winter where the weather gets warmer (2, 3, 4, 5, 6, 7, 10, 11)

summer The season after spring that is usually hot (2, 3, 6, 7, 8, 11)

winter The season after fall that is usually cold (3, 4, 9, 10, 11)

by Jose Aruego and Ariane Dewey

ScottForesman
A Division of HarperCollins*Publishers*

ISBN: 0-673-80101-2

Child-sized version of *Rockabye Crocodile* published 1993 by Scott, Foresman and Company, Glenview, Illinois.

Printed in the United States of America.
345678910-KPK-99989796959493

Scott, Foresman and Company

Editorial Offices:
Glenview, Illinois

Regional Offices:
Sunnyvale, California
Tucker, Georgia
Glenview, Illinois
Oakland, New Jersey
Carrollton, Texas

Two elderly boars lived in the jungle.
They were neighbors.

Amabel was cheerful and kind.

Nettie was mean and selfish.

One morning, Amabel trotted down to the river to fish. She was humming, HUM HUM HUM, as she passed a bamboo tree. It swayed to her tune and dropped two small fish into her basket. "Why, thank you," she said.

The bamboo replied with a shower of minnows.

Amabel filled her basket, said thank you again, and went on. She still needed a really big fish to fill her belly. Suddenly she stumbled over a crocodile.

"OH DEAR!" she cried.

"Good morning, Grandmother,"
growled the crocodile.
"Why don't you watch where you're going?"
"Excuse me," Amabel said. "I didn't see you.
I was looking for a fish for dinner."

"I'll catch one for you," said the crocodile,
"if you'll do something for me. Come into my cave."

A baby crocodile lay howling in a mud puddle
in a corner of the dark, dirty cave.

"Isn't he sweet?" said the crocodile.
"But he won't stop crying. Rock him to sleep
and you won't be sorry. I'll be right back."
And off she went.

The baby was muddy and cold, but Amabel held him gently and rocked and hummed, rocked and hummed. Soon the baby stopped howling and went to sleep.

The crocodile went to the deepest part
of the river and caught some eels and crabs
and a very large fish.

Then she wove a basket from river reeds, filled it, and returned to the cave.

"Here, Grandmother," she said.
"Come back whenever you want more fish."
"Thank you, I will," said Amabel.
"He's such a nice baby." Then she hurried home.

"Where did you catch all those fish?"
Nettie demanded.

"It all started with the bamboo tree," said Amabel.
"And then I met a crocodile." She told Nettie
the whole story while they shared the fish.

Early the next morning Nettie rushed to the river with a huge basket.

She shook the bamboo tree.

"Turn your leaves into fish for me," she ordered.

Nothing happened. She butted the tree hard.

The bamboo snapped back and sent her flying into a prickle bush. "**OOOUWHA!**" she screamed, and ran along the river bank.

"Where's that crocodile and her crybaby?" she snarled. The crocodile stuck her head out of the cave. "Oh, there you are," Nettie grunted. "Go fill this basket with eels, crabs, and big fish. **AND HURRY UP!"**

The crocodile was very angry, but she said, "Rock my baby to sleep and I'll do what you ask."

Nettie grabbed the baby and bounced him up and down. "What an ugly son. If I had one like you, I'd run," she crooned. The baby cried harder.

It wasn't long before the crocodile returned. She snatched back her baby and handed Nettie a basket. "Don't uncover this basket before you lock your doors and windows or the fish will escape," she growled.

Nettie grabbed the basket and was out the door and running home. "This food is all for me," she decided. "I won't share even a fish eye with Amabel."

Nettie sneaked into her house and bolted the door. She sealed the windows and stuffed grass into the cracks and holes. Finally she opened the basket.

WOOoooOoosh!

Out came spiders and scorpions, rats and bats.

Nettie huddled in a corner.

Next door, Amabel heard the noise. "What a ruckus," she thought. "I'd better see what's going on at Nettie's house." Amabel had to break the door down. The spiders, scorpions, rats, and bats rushed out of the open door.

"Oh, Amabel," Nettie cried. "I'm so glad to see you. I've been such a fool."

"Poor Nettie," said Amabel. "Come over to my house and have some tea and tell me all about it."

From that day on, Nettie and Amabel took turns caring for the crocodile baby and the bamboo tree, and the crocodile supplied them with all the fish they could eat.